MINDFULNESS
JOURNALING

Mindfulness Journaling

Tara Ward

ARCTURUS

Acknowledgements

Thanks to Coleman Barks for permission to include "The Guest House" on page 120, and to the Witter Bynner foundation for "Always We Hope" on 159.

This edition published in 2020 by Arcturus Publishing Limited
26/27 Bickels Yard, 151–153 Bermondsey Street,
London SE1 3HA

ISBN: 978-1-78888-583-6
AD006698US

Printed in China

Contents

Every morning we are born again. What we do today matters most.

Author's Note

Thank you for being here right now!

One of the loveliest aspects of mindfulness is that every moment is a new moment, regardless of what has happened, or what may happen. Mindfulness means "to be in the moment" and the more you practice it, the easier it becomes—and the better life feels.

So this book can help you to fully experience every moment in life, the difficult as well as the joyful, to feel more alive and more connected with yourself, and everything around you.

> *Mindfulness means giving
> your presence as a present.*

Introduction

Why mindfulness is important

Mindfulness can have a positive impact in every single aspect of your life because when you are spending time in the present, it means you are not reliving the past, nor anxious about the future—two places we tend to dwell in a lot! It means you can truly be there for others, as well as yourself. The sheer joy of really living every moment can only be experienced, not discussed, and discovering it for yourself is the perfect way to understand it.

So this journal is the opportunity for you to spend some quality time with a very important person in your life: YOU. Many of us rush around a lot, often doing things for others, and in the process we can neglect our own wellbeing. Yet spending a small amount of time alone, to recharge and relax, will make you even more effective when you re-emerge into the outer world again. So think of this as time that will allow you to become an even better version of you, because it's true.

And mindfulness isn't just about having reflection time and writing in your journal. As you will discover, it can be applied to all aspects of life, at any time. It's a way of being that can reduce stress and anxiety and enable you to connect fully with others.

How this book differs from my previous book, Mindful Journaling

In my earlier book, you take a journey into random ways of becoming mindful and explore what it means for you. In this book, there is a little more structure which allows you to choose an aspect of life to focus upon: Work, Play, Relationships, or Animals/Nature. There are also new tools for you to explore mindfulness with, including the addition of poetry, inspirational thoughts, and affirmations.

It doesn't matter in what order you read the books, simply that you enjoy them because we learn most when we are relaxed and engaged.

How to use this book

Every section has a mixture of suggestions as to how you can mindfully explore an area of your life. Some are creative and fun; others take you into deeper reflection and you may experience profound insights. Choose an exercise that feels right for you at the time, depending on your frame of mind.

Be honest as you write in your journal. Mindfulness is a very individual experience and there is no right or wrong response. It is also good to repeat an exercise occasionally and notice if you have a different outcome; it is very likely that you will, because our emotions and feelings change from moment to moment.

Many exercises only take a few minutes to do; others may last longer. Try to mix up your experiences and not just do the short ones! I know we are all busy, but this time for you is important and you deserve it.

The poetry can be spoken aloud or read silently. Take your time as you read the pieces and really allow yourself to absorb the words, to take in what you are feeling and thinking. It is the same with the quotes throughout this book. Read them slowly, a few times over; give yourself time to take them in.

Affirmations are amazing and their impact can be hard to explain until you try them. So when you come across an affirmation, say it out loud ten times to yourself. It doesn't matter if you don't believe it, because your brain will start to slowly re-program itself if you keep repeating it often enough. Once you get used to affirmations, it is fine if you come up with some of your own if you want to, but just remember they should always be phrased in the present and positive. So, for instance, you want to say: "I am relaxed" instead of "I am not tense" because, with

the latter, your brain will focus on the word "tense" and ignore the "not" in front of it. Likewise, you want to say "I create loving relationships" not "I will create loving relationships" because the latter implies a delayed action or state instead of a current one. Enjoy exploring affirmations.

In fact, please enjoy all aspects of this journal! Use different colored pens, scribble, draw, do whatever feels right for you. Add in pages if you want. It is your own special space to use as you wish.

Important points before you start

Being mindful can be unexpectedly emotional occasionally, so it's good to make sure you have some time when you won't be interrupted as you do these exercises. Many of them are short, so you only need to find a few minutes. Please avoid alcohol and drugs when practicing mindfulness, but do drink plenty of water!

Lastly, before you delve in, two final points:
1) Mindfulness is always enhanced when there is an awareness of your breathing first, so what follows on pages 10-11 is a very useful breathing exercise you can use before the start of any exercise.
2) You may well discover you want to hold onto your feelings at the end of an exercise, and that is wonderful. But occasionally you might feel emotional in some way and want to let go of this. The cleansing exercise on pages 14-15 can be used at any time. This exercise is also very useful if you want to let go of lots of thoughts running through your head and if you are distracted during mindfulness exercises.

Once you have read through and experienced these exercises, please start enjoying your mindful journal!

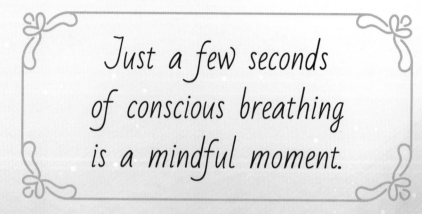

*Just a few seconds
of conscious breathing
is a mindful moment.*

Awareness of Breath Exercise

Either sitting or standing, take a few comfortable breaths. (If you are sitting, you may wish to close your eyes, but please keep them open if you are standing. Lowering your gaze to the ground works with both positions.)

Don't try to alter your breath in any way; simply observe it. Notice the cool air coming into your nostrils and making its way down into your lungs, then feel the warmth of the air as it is exhaled through your nostrils or mouth on the outbreath.

Enjoy this gentle cycle without any effort or without trying to change it in any way. You will notice your body begins to feel more relaxed and it may feel heavier. Some breaths are longer and shorter than others; this is normal.

Stay like this for as long as you can and then, slowly, open your eyes or lift your eyeline, to focus on something in front of you. Notice how heavy your feet feel on the ground. Wiggle your fingers and toes and give a little stretch before you continue with your day.

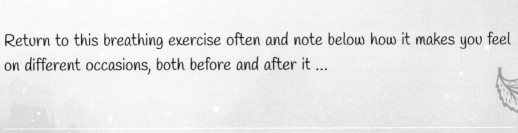

Return to this breathing exercise often and note below how it makes you feel on different occasions, both before and after it ...

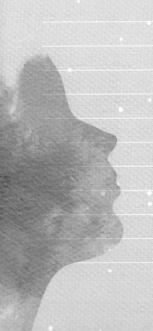

Breath Affirmation

Every breath I take
nurtures and uplifts me.

Repeat this out loud ten times and ask yourself how you feel. You might want to try breathing in and out between each repetition. Make a note of your feelings below. Try repeating this at least four or five times during a day, saying it ten times on each occasion. How do you feel at the end of the day?

_____

_____

_____

_____

_____

_____

_____

_____

_____

_____

_____

_____

_____

_____

_____

_____

_____

_____

_____

We cleanse our outer body regularly,
but how often do we remember to cleanse our inner body?

Cleansing Exercise

Sit or lie comfortably and close your eyes. Take a few comfortable, deep breaths and settle yourself.

Now ask yourself: What is your favorite body of water, the one to which you feel most drawn? Is it a lake, river, sea, stream, or waterfall? Perhaps it is a big bath, or a funky shower room, or even a swimming pool. Choose just one. It needs to be a place in which you feel happy to immerse yourself.

Now create the perfect image of that water in your mind. Picture where it is set, what surrounds it. Experience all the colors, sounds, and smells with it, even taste the air on your tongue. Enjoy the beauty and peace of it.

When you are ready, let yourself slip into the water and feel it relaxing and cleansing you. All your cares and anxieties are being washed away in the water. If your thoughts are jumbled or there are just too many of them filling your head, feel them all being washed away with the water until your mind feels empty and refreshed.

The more you see, hear, sense, smell, and taste the images, the more real the experience becomes and the more cleansed you will feel. Stay as long as you can, until you have to remove yourself and return to your present location.

Make sure your feet feel heavy on the ground and your body feels solid before you open your eyes and continue with your day.

Repeat this exercise as frequently as you can and try creating different locations and types of water. Make notes below about what you like most and why. Notice the more you return, the more "real" the experience becomes.

Cleansing Affirmation

All of me is
clean and refreshed.

After saying this out loud ten times, write down what you feel. Notice your response on different occasions. Remember it is fine to repeat your Cleansing Exercise as often as you wish.

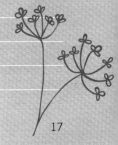

Life isn't about
making ourselves
into something else.

It is about
coming home
to who we really are.

What does this statement mean to you? Describe who you are below. Try to do this in one sentence. Don't think about it too much; simply take a deep breath and then write down the first thing that comes into your head. Return to this page and rewrite your description as you wish, as you experience different exercises in this journal ...

I am who I want to be.

1

Mindfulness at Work

Definitions of Work

- To function, especially properly or effectively

- Toil, labor, exertion, effort, slog

- To operate according to plan or design

- Activity involving mental or physical effort

- To produce a desired effect or result

- Something done or made as a result of an action

Which of those definitions are you drawn to, if any? Why? What do you agree/disagree with? Make a note of your initial thoughts. When you complete this chapter, return to these definitions again and notice if your attitude toward them has changed.

How to use this section

Work can mean many things,
so please use this section
of exercises in whatever way
you wish. For some, work might
mean how you earn a living; for others,
it could mean all the domestic tasks you
perform regularly, or the volunteer job you have.
So focus on whatever work area you want.

They are many attitudes you might have to work. It might
be a love/hate relationship; a way to survive; a main passion in
life. Perhaps it's a mixture for you.

This is the opportunity for you to discover your own personal
relationship to work and how it shapes who you are.

Go through the first few exercises in this section and simply
note how you are feeling and what you are thinking, without
trying to change or even analyse it in any way. Accept the flow
of thoughts and feelings and write them down afterward, without
judging or censoring them.

The later exercises give you the opportunity to understand
your feelings and thoughts on a deeper level. So work through
this section in order, taking your time, and enjoying the different
ways you can explore your attitude to work.

With all the exercises, before you start remember to focus on
your breathing for a moment or two to relax and ground yourself.

WORK
by Henry van Dyke

Let me but do my work from day to day,
In field or forest, at the desk or loom,
In roaring market place or tranquil room;
Let me but find it in my heart to say,
When vagrant wishes beckon me astray,
"This is my work; my blessing, not my doom;
"Of all who live, I am the one by whom
"This work can best be done in the right way."

Then shall I see it not too great, nor small,
To suit my spirit and to prove my powers;
Then shall I cheerful greet the laboring hours,
And cheerful turn, when the long shadows fall
At eventide, to play and love and rest,
Because I know for me my work is best.

Read this poem out loud, or silently, to yourself. Do it carefully, slowly, lingering over the words. What are you thinking? Notice your first feelings. It doesn't matter if they are negative or positive. Write them down. Then read it again. What jumps out at you now? Make a note. Be honest.

SIX O'CLOCK
by Trumbull Stickney

Now burst above the city's cold twilight

The piercing whistles and the tower-clocks:

For day is done. Along the frozen docks

The workmen set their ragged shirts aright.

Thro' factory doors a stream of dingy light

Follows the scrimmage as it quickly flocks

To hut and home among the snow's gray blocks.

I love you, human laborers. Good night!

Good night to all the blackened arms that ache!

Read these words slowly; take your time. Stop and breathe deeply between each sentence as you read it. Try reading it aloud. How does this make you feel? Are your emotions and thoughts different from the previous poem? If so, how? Why? Which piece resonates more with you? Why?

Work Affirmation

I value my work.
It sustains me
and others.

Say this aloud ten times and note your response below. It is fine to close your eyes and say the affirmation that way, if you want. Jot down the first things that come into your head, as well as your feelings about the affirmation. Then observe how you feel afterward: a few minutes later and then an hour later, or even at the end of that day. Repeat the affirmation before you go to sleep.

When you love what you do,
work becomes fun.

· · · · · ● · · · · ·

All work is an effort.
The trick is to find what
requires the least amount.

· · · · · ● · · · · ·

Every job, however small,
has purpose and value.

· · · · · ● · · · · ·

The best part of work
is when you finish.

· · · · · ● · · · · ·

Not all work is pleasurable,
but I can take satisfaction
from a job well done.

Read through each of the sentences slowly, breathing deeply and letting the words flow through you. How do you respond to each one? Write down your feelings against each quote.

Here are some very different pieces of music relating to work that you can look up and listen to, if you have the means to do so. Feel free to explore and add your own songs below.

Nine to Five
by Dolly Parton

The Flight of the Bumblebee
by Nikolai Rimsky-Korsakov

Heigh-Ho
(The Dwarf's Marching Song)
from Snow White & the Seven Dwarfs
by Frank Churchill

"A Hard Day's Night"
by The Beatles

Listening to music mindfully is different from having music as background noise. Make sure you can have a few minutes alone, then sit or lie, and really commit to listening and feeling the music. Pay particular attention to the lyrics, the beat, and the instruments. Literally breathe in the sounds and rhythm. Feel it filling you. Let your body relax and sway/move however you want through the sounds. Perhaps try having your eyes closed some of the time too. How does that affect your experience? What thoughts and emotions surface about work now?
Note the varying effects different pieces have on you.

Going Deeper

Mindfulness means
giving yourself
space to discover
who you really are.

✳ ✳ ✳ ✳ ✳ ✳ ✳ ✳
✳
✳
✳
✳
✳
✳
✳
✳

By now you will have accrued a selection of notes in your journal about how you feel and think about different aspects of work. Perhaps some of it has confused you; perhaps some of it is revealing. You may notice a theme running through your notes, or that you have a lot of different emotions going on. Have you remembered to use your Cleansing Exercise if you have been left with anything you don't want?

Now read back through your notes and choose just one aspect on which you'd like to focus. It might be a comment you made, or a feeling you had, or an unexpected thought that came to you. It can be big or small; it doesn't matter.

Take a few deep, comfortable breaths and ground yourself before you do this. Then read through the pages slowly, really absorbing the words you have written, or the pictures/symbols you've drawn. However you have expressed yourself thus far is right for you. As you do this, notice if your eyes are drawn to one page more strongly than any other.

When we are really "in the now" and being mindful, things have a habit of happening without us trying to force anything. So keep breathing as you read and reread your notes about work and wait until you "know" what you would like to focus upon.

Once you have chosen, continue with this section …

Take the work aspect you want to focus upon and either write it out below, or draw it, or do whatever you want to express it on paper. Again, take your time. Just let your energy flow.

First, simply gaze at what you've produced and let it sink in, remembering to breathe deeply as you do so. What are your initial thoughts and feelings? Write them down below.

Now try taking this aspect of work right inside of you. Let the words or images dance off the page and around you; even feel yourself swallowing the words or image, let it all go deep into you. Ask yourself what your body is telling you. What are you feeling? Where is the feeling in your body? Transfer your focus to that part of your body. What sensations are you having? What does it make you feel and think? Let the sensations wash over and through you and cleanse away anything you don't want to hold on to. Write down your experience.

Now ask yourself what you would like to do with what you have experienced. Is there any action you want to take? Anything more you need to explore? Give yourself time to breathe comfortably and check in with yourself. Ask yourself an appropriate question, such as "What do I want to do now work-wise?" Close your eyes. What images are you seeing? What sensations? Take your time. You may notice some insight or suggestion coming to you. When you are ready, withdraw your energy by focussing on your feet and how heavy they feel on the ground. Remember to make notes below when you finish. Cleanse away anything you don't want afterward.

Where has that journey taken you to now? It may have confused you or helped clarify something for you. Remember, with mindfulness, there is no right or wrong outcome. Write below what your relationship with work feels like now.

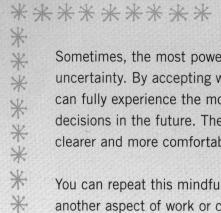

Sometimes, the most powerful way to be is sitting in indecision or uncertainty. By accepting where we are and what is happening, we can fully experience the moment and then be better placed to make decisions in the future. Then when we do move forward, we are clearer and more comfortable about what we really want.

You can repeat this mindful exercise at any time, focussing on another aspect of work or continuing your present train of thought to understand it better.

You are on a journey of exploration and discovery. There isn't a fixed end point and there is no right or wrong way to travel along your path. There is only the present moment and how you feel right now.

When Moments of Work are Mundane ...

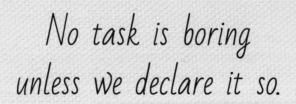

No task is boring
unless we declare it so.

✳✳✳✳✳✳✳✳
✳
✳
✳
✳
✳
✳
✳
✳

Lastly, before finishing this section, it seems practical to mention that for the majority of us there will be tasks needing to be done at some point that we will regard as mundane or tedious. Perhaps it may even be work you just don't want to do for some reason. Adopting mindful attitudes to these tasks can help enormously to make them more enjoyable. So how is this possible and what do we need to do?

Let me tell you about something I experienced many years ago. I was working in Nigeria and went into a ladies' toilet that could best be described as basic. I was in a cubicle when I heard a female voice starting to sing, softly at first and then with more power. The song was about the singer's gratitude for what she had in life. I emerged to discover an older woman cleaning the adjacent toilet on her hands and knees. She flashed me a massive smile and stopped singing long enough to say, "Good morning!" before continuing her work.

The experience humbled me because I couldn't see what she had to be so cheerful about. If my life was filled with cleaning these toilets, I was pretty sure I wouldn't be feeling grateful about it. Yet she radiated contentment. It was a stark lesson in understanding that one of the most unhelpful work attitudes we can have is dislike or resentment.

At the same time, mindfulness is not about denying emotions or beating ourselves up for having them. Being mindful is about discovering what we are truly feeling and thinking, accepting whatever that may be, and then choosing what we want to do about that situation.

This is where affirmations can be so powerful because they have the ability to help change our mind-set in a way that is empowering.

Any thought we have shapes our reality. Change our thoughts and our perception shifts too. The Nigerian cleaning lady taught me that.

So what can we do when we have a repetitive task that we would call "boring" or really dread doing, to shift it into something better through mindfulness?

Choose a task you really don't enjoy doing and then apply the next three exercises to it.

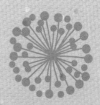

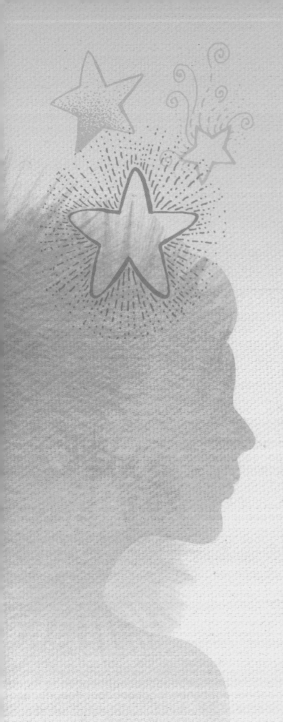

Before the Task

Before you do the task, close your eyes, breathe comfortably, and think about what the task is accomplishing; in other words, why are you doing it? What is the outcome or the purpose? What is the benefit from doing it? Who does it help? If not you, who? What would happen if you didn't do it? Why would that matter?

Next, ask yourself what you really feel and think about this task. Where is that feeling coming from? Where do you feel that reaction in your body? Breathe into it. What else is really going on for you? What is below that surface reaction? Take your time. Let yourself explore it. Cleanse away anything you don't want.

When you are ready, open your eyes and immediately write down what the exercise made you think and feel.

During the Task

You will want to be alone for this task, to enjoy the freedom of what you are about to do. You are going to perform it in a certain way. You are going to do every aspect of it slowly, very slowly. Whatever it is, stop to feel and examine thoroughly what you are doing as if it is the first time you have performed it. If appropriate, smell it or notice the sounds that come with this task. It might help to think of yourself as a child, alive with wonder and curiosity, experiencing something for the first time. If you are using particular items or tools, really think about where they come from, and how they were made. Who made them? And where did they make them?

As you do this, give thanks for your ability to do your task. It might be the dexterity of your body or mind or your own personal skill in performing it well. Really notice what parts of your body you are using; feel every tendon and muscle. What parts of your brain do you use? Think about how your brain is working right now to make this task happen.

Notice the effect of what you are doing and how your task is slowly getting completed. Appreciate the effect/benefit this will have on you or others. Continue your task slowly. Don't rush; don't hurry through the motions. Continue to observe the effects of doing something so mundane in this new way.

As you finish, give thanks for your capabilities, for the tools you have used, and for the outcome of your task. Really take the time to appreciate everything before you write down your experiences.

After the Task

What are you left feeling and thinking now? For some, depending upon the task itself, doing something simple in a totally mindful way like this can have a profound effect. You notice all sorts of things and have myriad feelings you didn't know were possible about a simple action. If you felt very little, that is fine too. That is your own personal experience.

Make notes about your responses to the task. Be honest.

You can repeat this exercise several times. Then try doing a different task and notice what happens.

Because we tend to do mundane tasks as quickly as possible, some of us might find doing the task slowly irritating or frustrating. That is all right as well. Slowing ourselves down in the middle of a fast-paced world can feel strange. The first time I did a simple task really mindfully, my brain kept saying to me, "Come on! Get on with it!" It doesn't do that so much today.

Make some notes below about your attitude toward mundane work now.

Keep doing different things this way when you can. It can be a small task: brushing your teeth, making the bed, taking the trash out! Keep experimenting with what mindful work means to you.

And, lastly, keep returning to the affirmation about work at the beginning of this section and notice how you feel the more you repeat it.

I do my work with love.

2

Mindfulness at Play

We all need to play,
children and adults alike,
because it nurtures us.

Why do we need mindfulness when we play? Surely when we are relaxing, we are naturally being mindful? Let's go straight into the exercise opposite and find out.

What does the word "PLAY" mean to you? Give yourself at least five minutes for this. Write the word below and then write or draw around it everything that it means to you. Remember to breathe deeply as you do this and enjoy the experience! Let your mind run free. Say the word "PLAY" as you write and draw—perhaps even hum or sing it! Use different colored pencils, or cut out and glue images onto the page. Anything and everything goes because this is your playtime …

Sit back and really examine what you have done. What is the first thing that strikes you? Write it down ...

Now close your eyes and ask yourself what this means to you in the context of play. Take some time to explore what you are feeling and thinking. Remember, nothing is right or wrong—it simply is. Sit comfortably, wriggle your body about to make sure it is relaxed, and breathe deeply. As you explore what this means to you, let yourself feel any sensation in your body that comes up. Go into the sensation and investigate. When you are ready, open your eyes and write down your feelings.

Now write below the word "FUN." What does this word mean to you? Express yourself however you wish and enjoy the freedom of anything being possible. Again, take your time. Perhaps you might want to stretch your arms upward and then outward, sweeping them around you; feel your lungs expanding. Repeat if it feels good.

Now look at what you have done. What leaps out at you straight away? How is it making you think and feel? Notice if it is similar to or different from your experience with the word "PLAY." Write below what you have found out.

Now, flick back and forth between your "PLAY" and "FUN" pages. Keep doing this, observing what is the same and what is different. Jot down how you feel about both words in relation to each other.

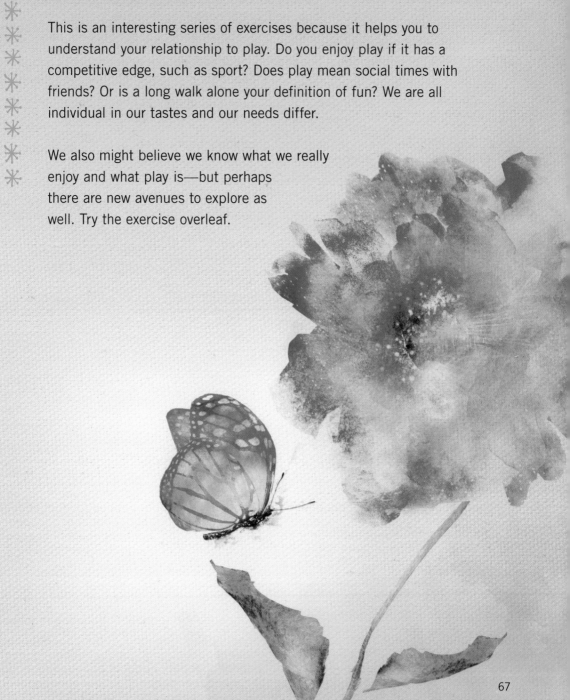

✳✳✳✳✳✳✳✳
✳
✳
✳
✳
✳
✳
✳
✳

This is an interesting series of exercises because it helps you to understand your relationship to play. Do you enjoy play if it has a competitive edge, such as sport? Does play mean social times with friends? Or is a long walk alone your definition of fun? We are all individual in our tastes and our needs differ.

We also might believe we know what we really enjoy and what play is—but perhaps there are new avenues to explore as well. Try the exercise overleaf.

Playful Objects Exercise

Gather together as many playful objects as you can. Lay them out in front of you. They could be games, ornaments, building blocks, toys, literally anything that means games, play and/or fun to you. (Avoid computer or electronic games for this exercise.) If you have young children, this might be easy to do; if you haven't, choose whatever items you have to hand.

Now take a few deep breaths and let your eyes scan the items. Which are you most drawn to? Which make you smile? Which do you most want to play with? Why? Pick up an item and really study it. What are you thinking/feeling about it? Where in your body are you feeling this? Try to describe the physical sensation it gives you.

_____

_____

_____

_____

_____

_____

If you can play with an item, do so now. Do it slowly and mindfully, being really aware of everything you are doing, and how it makes you think and feel. Pick up another item and play with it. How is that in comparison?

_____

_____

_____

_____

_____

_____

✳ ✳ ✳ ✳ ✳ ✳ ✳ ✳

✳
✳   When you've finished this exercise, place the objects back where
✳   they belong and notice if you feel differently about any of them.
✳
✳   Now try something very different. Choose an everyday object and
✳   pick it up. Examine it thoroughly, run your fingers along it, and ask
✳   yourself: "How can I play with this?"
✳
✳   This isn't a challenge; it's just a fun question to ask yourself.

What comes to mind? Write it down and even try playing the game if you
wish. If nothing occurs to you, that is fine too. Just make sure you write
down how you feel about this exercise.

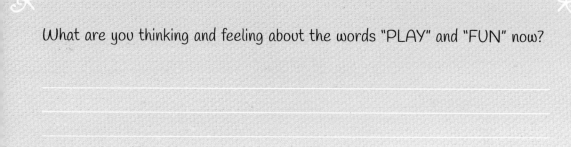

How we play and have fun reflects how we tend to live our lives. Some of us retain our childlike sense of fun and need to play throughout our lives; others may opt for more cerebral activities or sporting events for pleasure and relaxation. Remember, there is no right or wrong and there is no pressure to change. This is simply an opportunity for you to explore play and fun in a mindful way, and to understand yourself better.

What are you thinking and feeling about the words "PLAY" and "FUN" now?

Here are just a few of the
benefits experts say we get from
"playing." It:

- develops creativity

- fosters curiosity

- encourages stress-free learning

- creates laughter

- stimulates independent thinking

- increases sociability

- builds confidence

✳✳✳✳✳✳✳✳
✳
✳
✳　　It is a good list, isn't it?
✳　　But here's one of the best benefits
✳　　that few talk about …
✳
✳
✳

Playing is a mindful activity.

It's one of the few times in our lives when we can become totally
absorbed in something and therefore be fully "in the moment."
All our senses come alive at once when we allow ourselves to play.
Think about that as you look at the next two exercises.

I AM A CHILD
(Author unknown)

I am not built to sit still,
Keep my hands to myself,
Take turns, stand in line, be patient,
Or keep quiet.

I need motion, I need novelty,
I need adventure,
And I need to engage the world
With my whole body.
Let me play.
Trust me, I am learning!

Read this poem through slowly and notice how you feel. What does it make you think? How much do you relate to it? How do the sentiments make you feel? Write down your responses below. Be honest.

Listening mindfully to music about play can also help expand your relationship with it. Here are a few suggestions, but also experiment and find your own songs to listen to. Remember to stop, sit or lie, relax, and really listen to the music when you play it, letting the sounds and vibrations wash over and through you. I found so many pieces I didn't know when I did a search for "playful music." Enjoy exploring for yourself.

Fun, Fun, Fun
by The Beach Boys

Let's Go Fly a Kite
by The Sherman Brothers

Hoe Down
by Aaron Copeland

Bright Side of the Road
by Van Morrison

Walking the Dog
by George Gershwin

What kind of music makes you feel most playful? What feels most fun?
Why is that? Where do you feel it in your body? What is the sensation?

Play Affirmation

I enjoy playing
every day.

How does this make you feel and think after saying it aloud ten times? Write down your thoughts. Repeat this frequently and notice if your attitude changes.

Encouraging Mindful Play

A moment of play
every day makes us
more productive
and reduces stress.

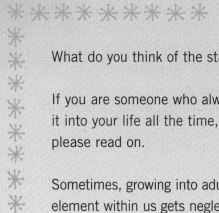

What do you think of the statement opposite?

If you are someone who always finds time for play and incorporates it into your life all the time, feel free to skip this section! Otherwise, please read on.

Sometimes, growing into adulthood can mean the "playful" element within us gets neglected. As we take on more and more responsibilities, through work, relationships, children, and home duties, fitting in fun and play might begin to seem too much of a luxury.

So this means we lose yet another opportunity for a mindful activity that could give us pleasure and help us to relax.

When you have some time, try the next exercise.

Playful Writing Exercise

You are simply going to answer the questions that follow, but you should do it in a fun and different way!

Start by asking yourself what color pen/pencil you normally write with. Choose another color or a different writing implement altogether. How does that feel in your hand?

Now choose somewhere different to sit/lie and do this exercise. It doesn't matter where, as long as you won't be disturbed. Where do you NOT usually write? Why? Try it now.

Next, you want to be comfortable and relaxed before you start. So settle yourself into your new place with your new writing implement. Perhaps you want to sit/lie in a different way too: Curl up on the floor or stretch out in some way. Take a few deep, comfortable breaths and feel yourself unwinding.

Enjoy being in a different environment. Notice how it makes you feel and what you're thinking. When you're ready, answer the questions overleaf.

Before you start, here's the twist. Place your writing implement in your other hand, the one you don't normally write with. Now start to answer the questions. It doesn't matter how messily you write. Take your time and write each word slowly, carefully. Enjoy the freedom of this new experience. Notice how writing with your other hand unleashes interesting thoughts.

What prevents me from having time to play? Be honest.

What can I do to change this? Create several solutions.

What kind of play do I want in my life today?

_____
_____
_____
_____
_____
_____
_____
_____

How will more mindful play benefit me personally?
List as many benefits as you can think of.

_____
_____
_____
_____
_____
_____
_____
_____
_____

This is how I will make it happen. Write or draw however you want to create your playful moments. Express yourself however you wish. If you want to, switch back to the hand you normally write with as you complete this last section. Note how switching back makes you feel.

✳ ✳ ✳ ✳ ✳ ✳ ✳ ✳
✳
✳
✳
✳
✳
✳
✳
✳

By the time you finish this section, I hope you will find you have a renewed interest toward mindful play in your life. You may want to make small changes, or they could be major ones.

You will notice I have asked you to avoid electronic games in this section. It is not because they don't have a place in playful activities, but because an increasing number of people have come to regard them as their main source of entertainment. There is so much more to play and relaxation than just this. Digital Detox is becoming an accepted expression and this section in particular is an opportunity for you to enjoy just that.

Whatever you have discovered so far about your attitude toward play in your life, come back and do these exercises again once you have explored new ways of playing.

Remember that with mindfulness your relationship to everything shifts "in the moment" and how you will feel one day may very well differ the next. That is one of the joys of mindfulness!

My playfulness nurtures me.

3

Mindfulness in Relationships

Being mindful with
those around us
means we see people
in a totally new light.

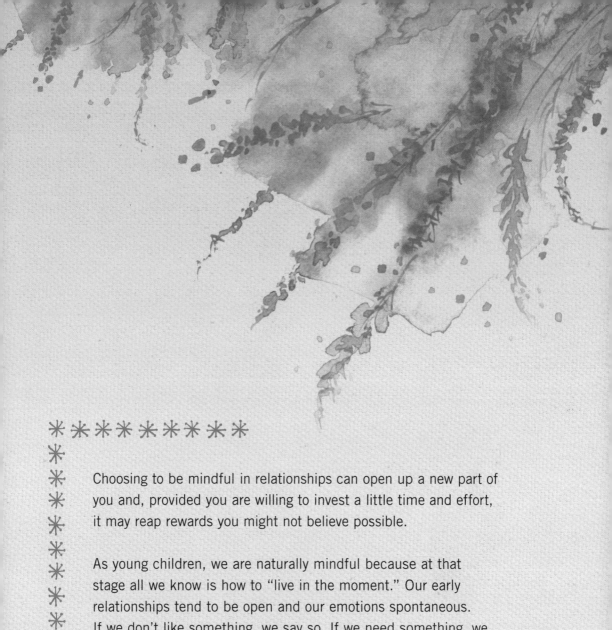

✳✳✳✳✳✳✳✳
✳
✳
✳
✳
✳
✳
✳
✳

Choosing to be mindful in relationships can open up a new part of you and, provided you are willing to invest a little time and effort, it may reap rewards you might not believe possible.

As young children, we are naturally mindful because at that stage all we know is how to "live in the moment." Our early relationships tend to be open and our emotions spontaneous. If we don't like something, we say so. If we need something, we ask for it directly.

We don't understand the concept of time and responsibility, so we don't try to organize or plan; we experience each moment as we go along and we tend not to worry about the future.

If you have ever held a young baby or rested them on your lap and watched them explore you, you will see mindfulness in action. Their interest in every part of you, their absorption in exploring what you are wearing, how they look at you with curiosity and wonder—it is truly mindful.

Now I'm not suggesting that as adults we should do the same thing, especially so overtly. This might unnerve a lot of people!

But the energy a young child brings to exploring and understanding others is very special because it is without judgment and assumption. That is the element that can shift our relationships into a healthy, mindful way of being.

So let's go straight into an exercise and start to explore this for ourselves.

Choose someone you are willing to focus upon for a few minutes. Avoid picking anyone with whom you might have a difficult relationship. You can save them for a later exercise! Now write below everything you think/feel about the person, regarding who they are and what they are like and how they might think/feel. Write as much as you like about any aspect of them. They won't see it, so you can be honest and you don't have to censor yourself in any way.

Now go through all your comments and, against each, write below how you know this about the person. It might be anything from "They told me" through to "I just feel it" or even "I don't know." Try to do this with every comment.

Notice what percentage of your comments seems to be true and what percentage is unknown or unsure. Now see if you can think of someone with whom you can do this exercise jointly. Ask them if they'd be willing to write down what they think of you and that you will do the same for them. Try the exercise again. You may not want to put the results of this exercise in the journal if you are sharing with someone, but if you do there is space below.

When you share with someone else, note down what you have discovered about each other. How much of it "matched" and how much was new to both of you? What have you learned from this exercise?

There is one other important element to consider. When you knew no one would see what you were writing down, how did that influence your ability to be honest? When you knew someone would read your comments, how much, if at all, did you censor yourself? Go back over both exercises to compare and make some notes below.

If you discovered that everything you thought about the other person was accurate—well done. You must be good at not judging others or making assumptions about them. Most of us will find we have jumped to conclusions or misinterpreted behavior in some way. As adults, we tend to make decisions about people very quickly, based on our experience of other acquaintances. We accrue a bank of knowledge as we go through life that we think helps us to understand others. Sometimes it is useful, but at other times it simply skews our impressions of people.

The way to connect and really understand others is to be in the moment through mindfulness. As you will be realizing, this is not our natural state with adult relationships, so please don't be too hard on yourself as you work through the following exercises. Try not to judge or criticize yourself if you find it difficult, and remember to acknowledge yourself when you have a real moment of mindfulness, however brief.

Photo Exercise

Choose a photo you like of someone you know, with whom you have a relationship. It doesn't matter what your connection with them is as long as you feel comfortable concentrating on them for a little while.

Prop the photo up in front of you, or hold it in your hands, whichever is more comfortable for you.

Now close your eyes and focus on your breathing. Feel your body relax, noticing how heavy it begins to feel. Enjoy the sensation of stopping to do this exercise and being able to leave your day behind for a while. Perhaps breathe in and say, "In," silently. Breathe out and say, "Out," silently. Repeat a few times.

When you feel nicely relaxed, open your eyes and look at the photo. What is the very first thing that comes to your mind as you look at this person? Ask yourself why that is. What is your second thought or feeling? Why?

Now look at the photo as if you have never seen it before. Study every aspect of this person really closely. Do this slowly and take your time. Notice what you are thinking and feeling.

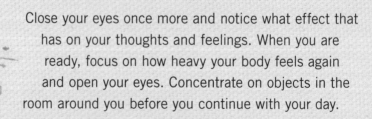

Close your eyes once more and notice what effect that has on your thoughts and feelings. When you are ready, focus on how heavy your body feels again and open your eyes. Concentrate on objects in the room around you before you continue with your day.

Make notes below on this exercise. For some, this can be an unexpectedly emotional experience. Remember to do your Cleansing Exercise if you need to wash away anything you don't want. Take your time writing down your thoughts and feelings.

Really seeing someone mindfully, as if for the first time, can be an unnerving experience, particularly if you think you know them well already. It can bring up all sorts of emotions, so please be kind to yourself if this is what happens to you. Alternatively, if you get very little from this exercise, that is fine too. Repeat it with another person in a photo, or do it on another day.

I suggest you do this with a photo first because it feels like a "safe" way to practice being mindful with someone. You may choose to do this exercise a few times on your own before you move on to further exercises.

Another important element of being mindful in relationships, apart from letting go of judgments and assumptions, is to be genuinely curious about someone. Part of the databank of information in our heads tells us that, if we have known someone for a long while, we might as well stop being curious about them because there is no need. This can happen particularly with family members as they are usually our longest relationships.

In the following pages are some "safe" ways to explore our ability to be curious.

Thumb Exercise

This sounds so simple, but please try it! Wash and dry both your hands thoroughly.

Now sit down, take a few comfortable breaths and lift up your right hand. Look at your right thumb. Just your right thumb, nothing else. Really look at it.

Notice each line and wrinkle: every single one. Look at your thumbnail closely and at the skin around it. Take in all the colors of your skin. Study your pores. What scars, if any, are there?

Move your thumb very slowly. How does it work? What muscles are being flexed as you do it? What happens to all the lines on your skin as you move your joints? How many tasks does this thumb perform for you every day? How often have you been appreciative of it?

Lift your thumb close to your ear and move it. Does it make any sound?

Sniff your thumb. Go on, sniff it. What does it smell like? Sniff the different parts? Do they have different scents?

Lick your thumb. Lick different parts of it. What does it taste like?

When you're finished, drop your hand back into your lap and focus on something else in the room for a moment before you pick up your pen and write down your experiences.

If possible, write down everything you notice and feel, being as specific as possible. Don't worry if it feels a little overwhelming, particularly if you have committed to this exercise and done it thoroughly. Just let your thoughts flow and write everything down.

✳✳✳✳✳✳✳✳
✳
✳
✳
✳
✳
✳
✳
✳

It can be an amazing experience to realize that we have never before properly examined this small part of us that we use daily. The thumb is an integral part of our hand and performs vital functions on a continual basis, yet how often do we stop and appreciate it? And when do we ever really look at it properly? This is just a tiny part of us. What about other fingers, our whole hand, our arm, and other parts of our incredibly complex body?

Are you feeling a little more curious and appreciative of your whole body now? Feel free to explore other parts of you this way and notice how it changes your relationship with them.

If you can take just a small part of your curiosity, and transfer it to wanting to understand and know others better, then you are well on your way to creating more mindful relationships.

And consider this: If you have just discovered that you don't even know a small part of your own body that well, what riches await you in really getting to know other people?

So let's move on to being mindful with others in the next exercise.

Interactive Exercise

This is an exercise you can do repeatedly that becomes easier the more you do it. Choose someone with whom you'd like to practice, initially not someone with whom you struggle. Give yourself an easy start!

The next interaction you have with them, whether it is face to face, over the phone, or even via email, commit to being curious about them. Greet them with the attitude in your mind of "I don't know much about you" or "I have too many assumptions and judgments, so I am going to let them go." If it is the latter, imagine being in your Cleansing Space and washing away those thoughts. If you have certain feelings before you interact with them, imagine those also being washed away before you contact them. You want to approach them with an open, uncluttered attitude. Notice how differently that starts your conversation.

Next, seek to find out one fact about the person that you didn't know by asking them an appropriate question. How does that shape what you now feel and think about them?

If you feel safe, share something about yourself too. How does that make you feel?

Finish the conversation on an appreciative note with them. Make sure it is sincere.

Now write down how you got on. What, if anything, was new about this exchange? How were you left feeling? What do you think the person felt at the end? Make notes about how easy/difficult you found it to let your assumptions and judgments go as you were speaking with them.

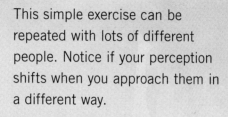

This simple exercise can be repeated with lots of different people. Notice if your perception shifts when you approach them in a different way.

If you have a mindful interaction and still end up with the same judgments and assumptions, ask yourself why. Constantly check out where your own feelings and thoughts are coming from.

When you are comfortable about having had a few mindful interactions with others, you can try moving into the last part in our Mindful Relationships section and see how the following exercises could help you with people who you find a bit more difficult.

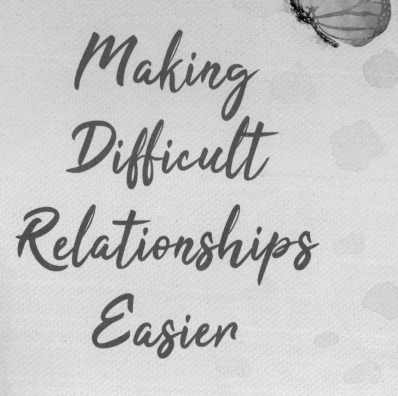

Making Difficult Relationships Easier

Relationship Affirmation

Every relationship is important.

Try saying the affirmation ten times and notice how you feel afterward. What thoughts are going around in your head? Make a note of them. Don't be surprised if you have a lot of thoughts! A simple affirmation like this can set off a lot of feelings. Take your time and try to capture everything. Remember to cleanse afterward if you need to. If you get very little the first time, try repeating the affirmation ten times again.

✳✳✳✳✳✳✳✳
✳
✳
✳
✳
✳
✳
✳
✳
✳

If you find yourself thinking, "Well, yes, BUT" after the affirmation, you won't be alone. Most of us have one or two people with whom we struggle in life, whether it is among our family, friends, or work circles. It is usually the person we try to avoid or need to take a deep breath and prepare ourselves for mentally before interacting with them. So let's see if mindfulness can help us to make that easier.

The following exercises can be quite emotional, so please make sure you do them when the time is right for you and when you have space to be alone and time to relax.

It is also important to acknowledge that being mindful doesn't mean every emotion is supposed to be a comfortable or happy one. Mindfulness is about accepting whatever we feel and working with it, not trying to bury it or block it out. The poet Rumi expresses it beautifully with the poem overleaf. Read it aloud a few times and let his words wash over and through you before you continue.

THE GUEST HOUSE

by Rumi
Translated by Coleman Barks

This being human is a guest house.
Every morning a new arrival.

A joy, a depression, a meanness,
some momentary awareness comes
as an unexpected visitor.

Welcome and entertain them all!
Even if they're a crowd of sorrows,
who violently sweep your house
empty of its furniture,
still, treat each guest honorably.
He may be clearing you out
for some new delight.

The dark thought, the shame, the malice,
meet them at the door laughing,
and invite them in.

Be grateful for whoever comes,
because each has been sent
as a guide from beyond.

Having troubled emotions or unsettling thoughts about others is a natural part of who we are and, once we accept them, it becomes easier to move through them.

It is also well worth remembering that ...

Every relationship can be strengthened when we commit to connecting mindfully with others.

So take a moment to pause and acknowledge yourself, accepting that you are being the best you can be and that you will continue in your quest to be this way.

Tricky Relationship Exercise

For this exercise, sit alone in a quiet room and, after a few minutes, imagine that the person with whom you struggle is sitting opposite you. If it feels more "real" to place an empty chair there before you start, please do so.

When you are ready, close your eyes and focus on yourself first. Feel your weight settle in the chair and become aware of your breathing. Notice how your shoulders drop down as they relax and how your body begins to feel heavier. Take your time.

Then, keeping your eyes closed, imagine the person you want to focus on is sitting opposite you. Remember, you have control and can let them go whenever you want to, so you have no need to feel daunted or overwhelmed by their presence. You can wash them away whenever you want.

What is the first thing you want to say to them? This is a safe place, so you can say whatever you want. What do they say back to you? (If they say nothing that is fine too.) What else do you want to say to them or ask them?

Remember to keep breathing and focus on how you are feeling as well as what you are thinking.

Two or three comments/questions may be enough the first time. When you have had enough, make them disappear in your mind's eye and then do your Cleansing Exercise straight away before you open your eyes and write in your journal.

Make a note of what you said/asked and what response you got. Also, jot down what you were feeling and thinking—and where that emotion manifested itself in your body. Lastly, check out with yourself how you feel about this person now. Cleanse again if you need to.

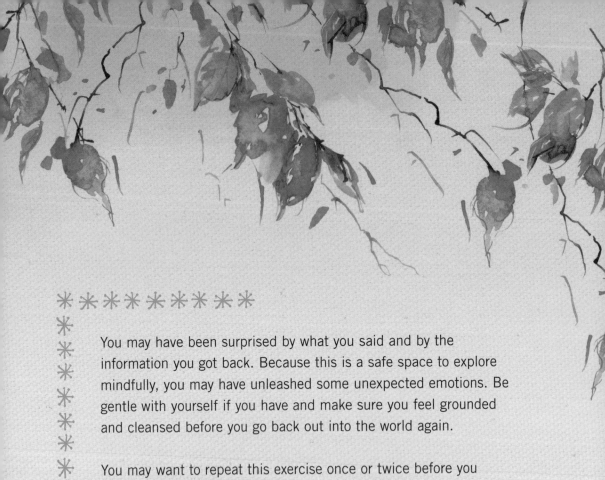

✳ ✳ ✳ ✳ ✳ ✳ ✳ ✳
✳
✳
✳
✳
✳
✳
✳

✳

✳

You may have been surprised by what you said and by the information you got back. Because this is a safe space to explore mindfully, you may have unleashed some unexpected emotions. Be gentle with yourself if you have and make sure you feel grounded and cleansed before you go back out into the world again.

You may want to repeat this exercise once or twice before you progress to the next stage. You don't have to set any time limits on your exploration because your feelings and thoughts need to unfold in a way that feels right for you, and that is a very individual experience.

You might discover that your next real interaction with this person has shifted in some unconscious way, simply because you have done this mindful exercise. That might be enough for you.

When and if you feel ready, try the next exercise, remembering to relax and breathe deeply before you start it.

Go back to the comments you made and write them down again below. Spread them out on the page.

After taking some deep and comfortable breaths, ask yourself why you said what you did and write down your response. Take your time as you go through each comment/question. Then go back to the first comment and ask yourself what it would take for you to say this to the person's face. What would the circumstances need to be? How could you make that happen?

✳✳✳✳✳✳✳✳

When you have finished that exercise, you might find yourself committed to having a deeper conversation with the person in question. You might even discover you can't wait to do so. If you feel hesitant, ask yourself why and what you could do to make it feel easier.

If you have found these exercises hard to do and unrewarding, try strengthening the image you have in your mind's eye of the person sitting in front of you. Imagine how they are dressed, their scent, how they sound. This requires more effort for some people.

These are deceptively simple but very powerful exercises and should be undertaken with care. Make sure you are in the right frame of mind before doing them.

On pages 128-9 is one last exercise for making a relationship easier. This may feel "lighter" to you and you might enjoy exploring it!

Regarding the person you struggle to get along with, answer the following questions:

What do we already have in common?

_____

_____

_____

_____

How could we enjoy that more?

_____

_____

_____

_____

What values do we share?

_____

_____

_____

_____

How could that play a more important part in our relationship?

_____

_____

_____

_____

What fun, if any, do we have together?

_____

_____

_____

_____

How could we create more?

_____

_____

_____

_____

What do I still not know about them that I'd like to know?

_____

_____

_____

_____

How could I find out in a way that is appropriate?

_____

_____

_____

_____

Perhaps you found that exercise easier, and more fun! You might even want to re-read your notes from the previous Mindfulness at Play section and see how you could bring more of those elements into your relationships. Sometimes we convince ourselves that relationships are hard work, when really we just need to increase the number of playful moments.

Whatever you experience personally with these mindfulness exercises, the most important way to be mindful with others is to drop your judgments and assumptions and to be genuinely curious about them. Then it becomes easier to listen and empathize with them.

Here is one last thought to leave you with in our Mindful Relationships section. When you are mindful in your relationships and respond to someone purely "in the moment," this is what happens …

> *Every interaction*
> *you have with someone*
> *creates a new*
> *relationship.*

I bring mindfulness to all
my relationships.

4

Mindfulness with Animals and Nature

To experience a moment
of true mindfulness,
take a walk among nature
or stop to observe an animal.

✳ ✳ ✳ ✳ ✳ ✳ ✳ ✳ ✳
✳
✳
✳
✳
✳
✳
✳

Some of you may be wondering why I have included a section on animals and nature. Work, play, and relationships seem the more obvious aspects of life to focus upon, so how can the natural world be relevant?

In many ways, this section helps to tie together the other three and is one you can come to repeatedly when you want to fit more mindfulness into your life in a simple and pleasant way. These exercises may also be helpful if you've found something in another section a little overwhelming and need to recharge or reorient yourself.

While we might want to incorporate more mindfulness into our everyday life, my experience has been that it isn't a habit we adopt easily. Modern society seems structured in a pressured way, encouraging us to move quickly from one thing to another and, in many cases, our attention span is growing shorter because of this.

Yet taking even a small break from our hectic schedules to enjoy a mindful moment in nature and/or observe the behavior of an animal has benefits that affect our daily lives.

To give an example, just now I stopped to have a mindful moment and observed a little spider crawling down the sleeve of my sweater.

I am glad I was able to release it safely outdoors and that happened only because I stopped to have a moment's pause in my busy day. This is one tiny way to show how a small moment of mindfulness can create a positive ripple.

So please do try some of the exercises in this section and see the effect it has on you and on your relationship with mindfulness.

Let's start with a simple exercise.

Leaf Exercise

Find a leaf. It can be indoors or outdoors, attached to a plant or tree, or fallen on to the ground. It doesn't have to be beautiful or special—any leaf will do.

Now examine it closely. Look at its shape, notice all its different colours and hues, feel its texture, sniff it, think about where it has come from, and how it has grown.

Now put the leaf down, out of your eyeline, and write down what you can remember about it.

_____

_____

_____

_____

_____

_____

_____

_____

When you have done that, return to the leaf and examine it closely again. What do you notice this time? Take a few deep breaths to focus, ground yourself, and keep observing. What more are you discovering? Have the leaf in front of you as you make notes this time. Glance over at it as you write.

_____

_____

_____

_____

_____

_____

_____

✳ ✳ ✳ ✳ ✳ ✳ ✳ ✳
✳
✳
✳
✳
✳
✳
✳
✳

This easy exercise can produce some surprising results. Even when we think we are being observant, often we miss things. It is not easy to be fully mindful, especially in the beginning. Being really "in the moment" with something or someone means filtering out distractions.

There is something about being at one with nature and animals that makes that transition a little easier, which is why it is important to find time to commune with both.

When you were focussing on the leaf, how much time did you spend thinking of other things? When we immerse ourselves fully in nature, other thoughts, anxieties, and distractions tend to fall away.

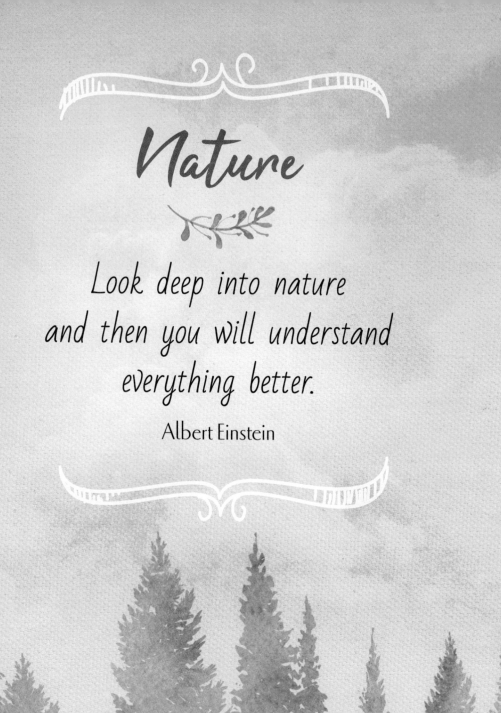

Nature

Look deep into nature
and then you will understand
everything better.

Albert Einstein

THE OCEAN
by G. Ward

Along the soft warm path
I walk among the pines.
The wind of speaking words
Enters into my heart.
A peacefulness I feel
Surrounding like a hug.

The path goes steeply down,
Ahead in view the sea.
Along the shore I stroll,
The waves around my legs.
With playfulness I splash;
My joyful laughs ring out.

Imagining to be
A seagull flying free
Anxieties leave me.
Calmness bestills my heart.

The afternoon passes
Serenity sweeps in.
To be near the ocean
Is life itself indeed!

Read this poem slowly and notice how it makes you feel and think.
What moments in it resonate with you the most? Why? What other bodies
of water are you drawn to? Where else in nature do you like to walk, and
how does it make you feel?

Nature Journey Exercise

Being mindful among nature is a beautiful journey of discovery and there are endless ways to do it. Once you start, you'll never want to stop. Here are a few suggestions for exercises. Do as many as you can and make notes about your experiences. Remember to do these slowly, mindfully. When we rush, we miss the art of mindfulness and end up "doing a task," which is the opposite of "being in the moment." Remember your breathing through all the exercises as well. Take deep, comfortable breaths and feel yourself relaxing before and during the exercises.

Watch an insect moving:

_____

_____

_____

_____

Listen to birdsong:

_____

_____

_____

_____

_____

Lie on your back and look up at the sky:

_____

_____

_____

_____

_____

Hug a tree:

_____

_____

_____

_____

_____

Walk barefoot in sand or grass:

_____

_____

_____

_____

_____

Study any flower closely:

_____

_____

_____

_____

_____

Focus on the sounds of rustling trees:

_____
_____
_____
_____

Eat a piece of fruit really slowly and carefully, chewing many times before swallowing:

_____
_____
_____
_____

Take a blade of grass or a leaf and brush it very slowly up and down your arm or leg:

_____
_____
_____
_____

Sit by any body of water and look at it as if for the first time. How would you describe it?:

_____
_____
_____
_____

Find a flower that has a strong scent and breathe it in slowly.
Repeat several times:

_____

_____

_____

_____

Take a walk among nature and challenge yourself to use all your senses.
What can you hear, see, smell, taste, and sense?

_____

_____

_____

_____

When outside in rain, wind, sun, or cloud, lift your face to the elements and allow
yourself to feel them on your skin:

_____

_____

_____

_____

Run your fingers through soil, sand, or grass. Concentrate on the sensations
and sounds:

_____

_____

_____

_____

The more you try these exercises, the more you will want to explore. Use this page to write down any other moments of nature-filled mindfulness that you discover for yourself and the effect they have on you. Or write down what you enjoy the most and why.

If you live in a big city, it can be hard to find the opportunity for nature appreciation. If you can't go outdoors into nature, listen mindfully to music or sounds that reflect it. It is great to do this in a break at work, as it can help you to unwind quickly. Here are a few suggestions for ambient soundtracks:

Forest Birdsong
by The Silent Watcher

Rain
by Relaxing White Noise

Sounds of Birds
by Bird Songs

Ocean Waves
by Sea Waves Sounds

Nature Sounds of a Forest
by Johnnie Lawson

You can always bring a little nature into your own home. Growing herbs on a windowsill, for example, can be a wonderful, mindful activity. Watching plants as they grow, enjoying their different scents, picking them carefully, and using them in cooking are mindful delights. Some, such as mint, are usually easy to grow and can yield a lot of leaves quite quickly. Try acquiring a few herbs and see if they improve your mindfulness appreciation.

 Make notes below of any herbs you grow and which you enjoy most.

If growing herbs isn't an option for you, try buying some essential oils. Keep a pure essential oil (not synthetic) in small quantities around you. Even a few drops dabbed on a tissue beside you can encourage you to slow down when you work, to breathe deeply and be more mindful. Lavender is particularly good for relaxing, rosemary is uplifting, and peppermint is great as a digestive aid. (If you are pregnant, dealing with depression, or have any other condition, be careful of any warnings linked to certain oils and check before using them.)

Make a note of any oils you experiment with below.

Nature has so many beautiful gifts
to offer us. One of the ways you can
deepen your mindful connection with
it is to consider how certain things
happen in nature.

Any of the exercises above can become
more intense when you ask yourself
"Why is this so?" or "How has this
come about?" It helps you to focus and
can lead to deeper connections.

Another benefit of this is that it can
lead to greater appreciation of so many
things in life. Mindfulness has a habit
of doing that anyway, but appreciation
of nature can take joy and wonder to
another level entirely.

Animals

· · · · ● · · · ·

When you extend the
circle of your compassion
to all living things,
you will find peace.

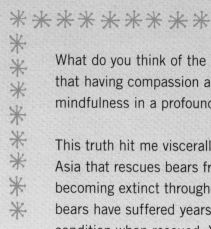

What do you think of the quote opposite? I would extend it to say that having compassion and understanding for animals teaches us mindfulness in a profound way.

This truth hit me viscerally when I became involved in a charity in Asia that rescues bears from bile farms, a practice which is slowly becoming extinct throughout Asia. Most of Animals Asia's rescued bears have suffered years of extreme torture and are in a pitiful condition when rescued. Yet the charity has had repeated success with turning hundreds of these bears back into playful, relaxed, and contented creatures. They could be missing limbs or teeth and have been through great psychological trauma, but most of them revert to their natural state of mindfulness in time—living in the present—in conditions that allow them to play and forage without fear.

As humans, I believe we find that more difficult to do because we tend to remain connected more to our past, particularly with trauma; that's why PTSD (Post Traumatic Stress Disorder) has become a widespread condition which can lead to depression. Likewise, many of us can be worried about our future with a lot of "what ifs" running through our minds and that can end up creating anxiety and stress. These are two examples of how we find mindfulness difficult because we can focus too much on the past or the future instead of the present.

This is why time with animals can be such a wonderful lesson in mindfulness for all of us. We can practice mindfulness with our domestic animals, whatever they may be, and also among wild animals. So let's look at how we can learn from them.

A good place to start is simply through observing them. If you have a pet, simply spend a few minutes watching it. It can be eating, washing, looking at something, or even sleeping. Just a few moments really connecting with its energy will help you to understand how it lives mindfully because, whatever it is doing, it commits to it totally. It is amazing how absorbed a cat can be as it cleans a patch of fur, as if it is the only thing that exists in its universe, or the way a dog chases a stick or a ball oblivious to anything else. How often do we emulate that single-mindedness? Make a note of your first animal observation and what you have learned. Ask yourself what circumstances you could find yourself in where you might mirror that mindful attention to something.

Another useful way to connect with animal behaviour is to go to a park or a well-run animal sanctuary and spend time watching. (It is not always helpful to go to zoos as the conditions in which animals are often kept can unfortunately lead to stressed behavior such as pacing or cage rattling, where their natural mindful instincts are stifled and distorted. When you study mindfulness in animals, you become more aware of when this is happening, so try to choose more natural habitats whenever possible for this observation.) Make notes about what you learn.

There are also lots of opportunities to watch animals online. I don't mean it in the sense of flicking through comedy compilations of animal antics, but rather how you can choose an animal subject and commit to watching it mindfully, fully absorbing the animals' behavior and energy. Watch their movement and how their single-mindedness informs everything they do. Try choosing a wild animal and see how the experience differs for you.

It can be fascinating to choose a small insect, such as an ant or beetle. Watch as they go about their work, focussing only on their immediate surroundings and their task. How often do you achieve this yourself? After you've been concentrating on tiny creatures, notice how you feel when you pull yourself back into the bigger, wider world. What thoughts go through your mind?

Animal Connection Exercise

Here is a playful way to explore animal mindfulness and how you connect with it. Settle yourself comfortably somewhere quiet, close your eyes, and focus on your breathing for a few moments. Then ask yourself what animal you feel most drawn to or connected with. You might find an answer that surprises you comes to you immediately, or it might take a while for something to happen.

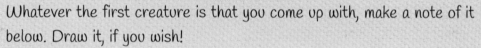

Whatever the first creature is that you come up with, make a note of it below. Draw it, if you wish!

Now spend some time over the next week or so seeing what you can find out about this animal. Make notes about it, paste in some pictures of it if you want, spend time looking at it in whatever form you have available to you. Enjoy exploring this creature. Look up unusual facts about it; challenge your present understanding of it.

Fill the next two pages with anything and everything you find out as well as how it makes you feel and think. There is no right or wrong way to do this; just enjoy it! If you decide you want to explore another animal too, do that. There are no rules!

My animal

Here is another way to work with the mindfulness of animals. When you feel stuck with something, it could help you. For instance, the next time you find yourself in a relationship or situation you find difficult, ask yourself this. What animal am I being? Why? What animal is the situation or other person? Why? Who would I need to become to handle this better? Then focus on the creature you would like to become, immersing yourself in their energy, and make notes about how you want to change. Then sit quietly, breathe, and ask yourself how to implement this. You may be amazed at what unfolds for you.

So what have you learned now through your exploration of animals? We can connect with mindfulness through many different paths and I have discovered over the years that animals can be a lovely way to do this.

There is something poignant and a little sad about the fact that we are born understanding mindfulness, just as all animals are, and yet as humans we end up losing this ability and having to be re-taught. Animals can help us in this respect.

If connecting with animals doesn't resonate with you, that is fine, but do try a few of these exercises before you dismiss it. If we are not brought up with animals, it can take longer for those connections to be made, but we can still create them over time.

In Closing

We are coming to the conclusion of this book, except of course this journal never has to finish because you can always return to any section when you wish and explore it again.

I recommend particularly that you return to the very first exercise in this journal, where you describe who you are. Notice how it changes over time.

The joy of mindfulness lies in neverending discovery and that is partly why I love it so. It is not about getting somewhere; it is about enjoying every day as it comes along. Of course it is good to have goals, but never to the exclusion of living each, individual moment along the way.

The more I slow down to savor every day, the better it makes me feel, even when life is challenging. I hope this is what you discover too in your own personal mindful journey.

Here is a Lao Tzu poem as a final poetic reflection on mindfulness …

ALWAYS WE HOPE
by Lao Tzu

Always we hope
Someone else has the answer
Some other place will be better,
Some other time it will all turn out.
This is it.
No one else has the answer
No other place will be better,
And it has already turned out.
At the center of your being
You have the answer,
You know who you are
And you know what you want.
There is no need
To run outside
For better seeing.
Nor to peer from a window.
Rather abide at the center of your being;
For the more you leave it, the less you learn.
Search your heart
And see
The way to do
Is to be.

To close, here is the last affirmation I would like to offer you. When we live a life with gratitude, it makes everything we experience easier to accept.

Thank you for being here through these pages and may your future be filled with many enlightening and uplifting mindful moments.

Affirmation

I am grateful for all I have.